JEDEDIAH SMITH

Mountain Man

by Dennis Fertig

Boston, Massachusetts
Chandler, Arizona
Glenview, Illinois
Upper Saddle River, New Jersey

Illustrations
Opener, 1, 2, 3, 4, 9, 12, 14, 15 John White; 13 Joe LeMonnier.

Photographs
Every effort has been made to secure permission and provide appropriate credit for photographic material.
The publisher deeply regrets any omission and pledges to correct errors called to its attention in subsequent editions.

Unless otherwise acknowledged, all photographs are the property of Pearson Education, Inc.

Photo locators denoted as follows: Top (T), Center (C), Bottom (B), Left (L), Right (R), Background (Bkgd)

Opener: (Bkgd) Prints & Photographs Division, LC-USZ62-108523/Library of Congress; 3 Dynamic Graphics, 2007/
Thinkstock; 5 Prints & Photographs Division, LC-USZ61-1473/Library of Congress; 6 Curtis (Edward S.) Collection, Prints &
Photographs Division, LC-USZ62-130160/Library of Congress; 7 Stockbyte/Thinkstock; 8 Hemera Technologies/Thinkstock;
10 Comstock/Thinkstock; 11 Prints & Photographs Division, LC-USZ62-113676/Library of Congress.

ISBN-13: 978-0-328-67650-7
ISBN-10: 0-328-67650-0

3 4 5 6 7 8 9 10 V0FL 15 14 13 12

Grizzly Attack!

In 1823, a grizzly bear suddenly attacked a group of fur **trappers** led by Jedediah Smith. The trappers shot the bear, but Smith was seriously injured. What should they do? Smith asked for a needle and thread. He then ordered a man to stitch him up. Amazingly, Smith was soon well enough to travel.

Why did Smith risk his life in such a dangerous place? This is the story of Jedediah Smith. He was one of America's greatest **explorers**.

In the early 1800s, many people were inspired by the journey of explorers Lewis and Clark.

Inspired by Lewis and Clark

Jedediah Smith was born in 1799 in New York. His family moved to Pennsylvania and then Ohio. Smith grew up hunting and fishing.

Young Smith read the journals of Lewis and Clark. From 1804 to 1806, these men had led a group that explored the new western lands of the United States. Their journals were filled with rich details that described all that they had seen. They inspired many people, including Smith.

A Young Trapper

When Smith was 22, he left for St. Louis with the hope of exploring the West. He also hoped to earn a living trapping beavers. Beaver fur was used to make all kinds of clothing. It was so valuable it was called "brown gold."

Then Smith saw an ad in a newspaper. A trapper named William Ashley was hiring men. Whoever took the job would face many challenges.

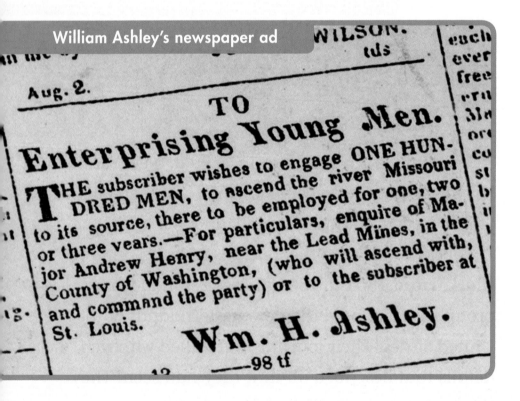

William Ashley's newspaper ad

Aug. 2.

TO
Enterprising Young Men.

THE subscriber wishes to engage ONE HUN-
DRED MEN, to ascend the river Missouri
to its source, there to be employed for one, two
or three years.—For particulars, enquire of Ma-
jor Andrew Henry, near the Lead Mines, in the
County of Washington, (who will ascend with,
and command the party) or to the subscriber at
St. Louis.   Wm. H. Ashley.
——98 tf

Trappers traveled on boats designed for travel on shallow rivers.

Smith answered the ad. In the spring of 1822, he joined trappers heading up the Missouri River.

Trappers were called mountain men. A rough bunch, they risked their lives for brown gold. Then, they spent all their earnings. However, Smith was different. He didn't share these bad habits. He carefully saved his money. Smith could read and write. Later, he even became a good mapmaker.

A Battle

Lewis and Clark had traveled up the Missouri River. They had hoped it was part of a water route to the Pacific Ocean. It was not. In fact, no such water route existed.

However, trappers still traveled on the Missouri, where many Native American people lived. Some of these people didn't trust trappers. Not all trappers dealt with them fairly. In the spring of 1823, Ashley's trappers got into a fight with the Arikara people. People were killed. Smith fought hard to protect the trappers.

This early 1900s photograph shows an Arikara man named White Shield.

Today, much of the Badlands is part of Badlands National Park.

Becoming a Leader

Afterward, Ashley left the Missouri River area. He made two groups of trappers. He would lead one group, and Smith would lead the other. Ashley trusted Smith.

Smith led his group through the Badlands, now part of South Dakota. In the 1820s, only Native Americans had seen this **arid** land. It was hot, dry, and little grew there. The trappers struggled to survive.

The Rockies were extremely difficult to cross.

Several weeks later, Smith's group came upon the grizzly bear. Smith's bravery and quick thinking saved his life.

That winter, the trappers stayed with a Native American people called the Crow. The trappers were looking for a way to cross the Rocky Mountains. The Crow people said they knew of a pass. They said it crossed the rugged mountains.

Smith Opens the Way West

That spring, Smith found the mountain pass. He was the first explorer to map the route. It became known as South Pass. Later, it became part of the Oregon Trail and was used by **pioneers**.

In 1826, Smith attended a **rendezvous**, a gathering of trappers. While there, he bought Ashley's business. For the next four years, Smith explored the wonders of the West.

At a rendezvous, trappers traded their furs for money and supplies.

To California

When Smith and his group left the rendezvous, they began moving west toward California. They soon entered a dry, rocky **desert**. This was the edge of the area called the Great Basin. Very little grew there. Smith called it "the country of starvation."

Today, the Great Basin is part of Utah and Nevada.

A valley in California

The group then entered California. They were the first Americans to reach California by land. The trappers made their way to a valley near what is now Los Angeles.

California was then part of Mexico. The Mexican government feared that Smith was an American spy and told him to leave. His group left Los Angeles, but not California. Instead, they headed north to trap beavers.

California Once Again

The trappers trapped many beavers that winter. They hoped to sell the furs at a rendezvous. However, the horses couldn't carry the enormous load through the spring snow! Smith set up a camp. Then, with two men, he headed off to the rendezvous, leaving the rest of the group behind. The three men were the first Americans to cross the Sierra Nevada mountains. Next the men crossed the Great Basin Desert. This was another first for non–Native Americans. Ten days later, Smith left the rendezvous with men and horses and began his return trip. He wanted to get back to the men who had been left behind.

Exploration by Jedidiah Smith

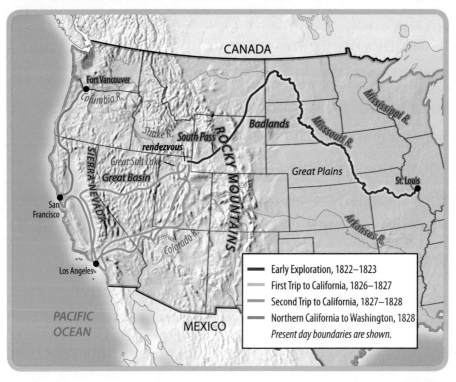

Smith and his party didn't find friendly Native Americans. Mojave people, angry with other trappers, attacked them. They killed more than half of the trappers. Smith, however, survived.

Smith and the other surviving trappers struggled to cross the desert again. In California, Mexico again ordered Smith out. And, again, the trappers went farther north instead.

The End of Many Trails

Smith's group traveled along the Sierra Nevada Mountains. Smith hoped they could find a way to get across the mountains and get to the coast. They were not able to find a way. The group continued traveling farther north instead. Finally, they reached what is now the state of Washington. This trip by land from California to Washington was another first for Americans.

Then disaster struck once again. A Native American group attacked the expedition, and 15 trappers died. Only Smith and three others reached safety.

Hundreds of thousands of pioneers would later travel on the Oregon Trail, following a route partly mapped out by Smith.

Finally, a weary Smith sold his business. However, in the spring of 1831, he made one last trip. While scouting alone, Smith ran into a group of Comanche Native Americans. Shots were fired, and two people died. Smith was one of them.

Smith died young. Yet, like Lewis and Clark, he bravely traveled to places few had seen. He mapped his routes and wrote about his trips. He urged others to follow him. Later, pioneers who traveled west often followed Smith's trails. Jedediah Smith was one of America's great explorers.

Glossary

arid dry

desert an area that gets little rain or snow

explorer a person who travels to new places

pioneer one of the first settlers in a place

rendezvous a gathering of mountain men, or fur trappers

trapper someone who traps, or catches, animals and sells their fur